AF552707

DEDICATIONS

For my husband, Hugh, whose patience, sensitivity and poetic spirit inspire me always. And for Ameeta, whose knowledge and love of Indian culture guided us, and enriched both our travels and the creation of this book.
– Melba Levick

For Nilou and Mitch, my guides and extraordinary friends throughout my travels in India.
For Melba Levick, who has caringly taken me under her wing and introduced me to a whole new exciting world of books and writing.
– Ameeta Nanji

For the unnamed women and men who appear in this book and for their dignity, beauty, skill and constant inspiration.

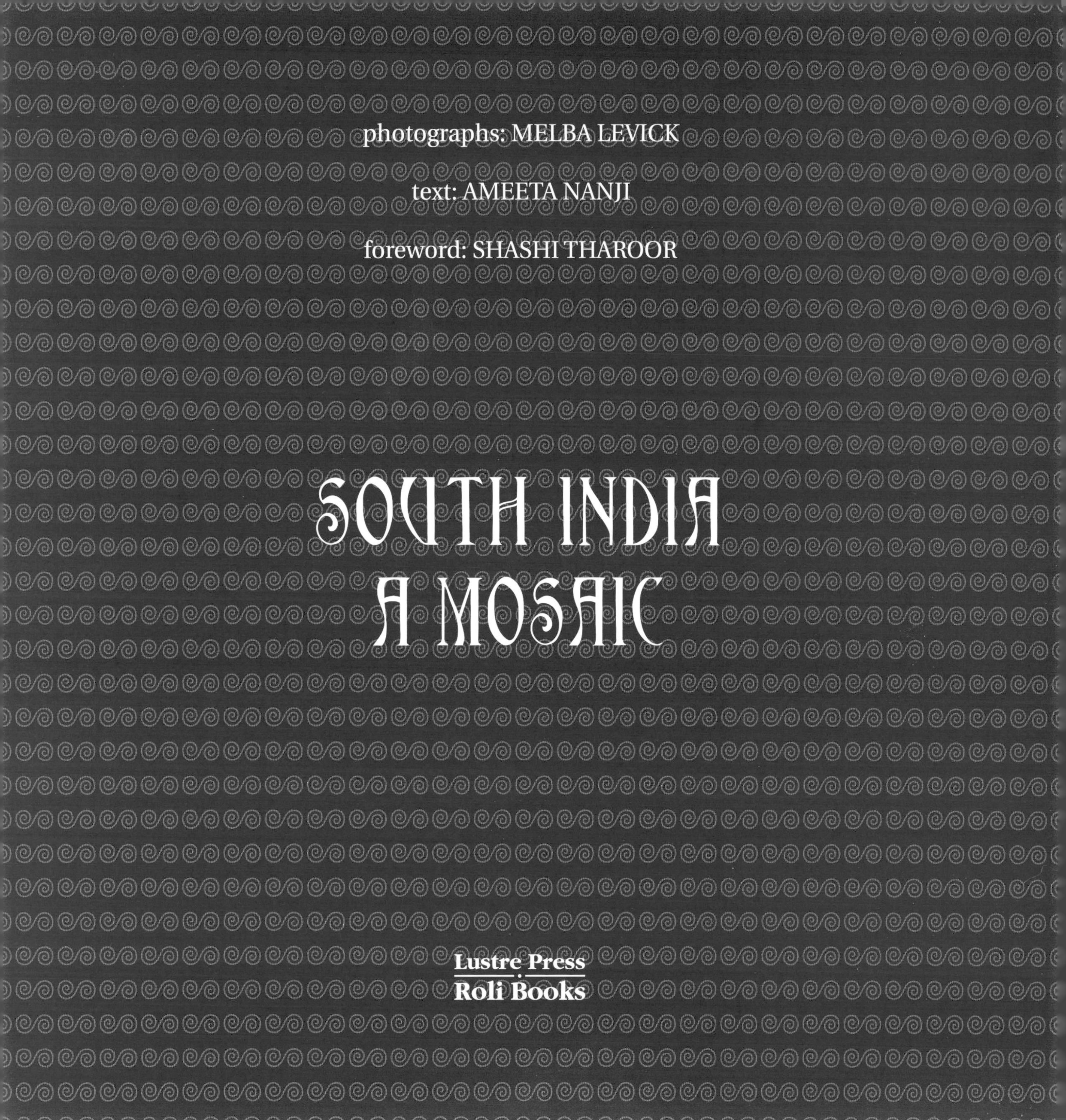

photographs: MELBA LEVICK

text: AMEETA NANJI

foreword: SHASHI THAROOR

SOUTH INDIA A MOSAIC

Lustre Press
Roli Books

CONTENTS

9 **ACKNOWLEDGEMENTS**
10 **INTRODUCTION**

16 **BACKWATER LIFE**

24 **DEVOTION**
32 Sacred Marks
36 Dance
44 The Temple
48 Meenakshi Madurai
56 Roadside Shrines

60 **ARCHITECTURE & DESIGN**
62 Chettinad Style
72 Dwellings
78 Details
80 Living South
84 Fanciful Facades

86 **THE STREET**
88 Bazaars and Markets
94 Street Food and Spices
100 Flowers
106 Banners and Cut-Outs

110 **HANDWORK**
118 Coconuts and Coir
122 Silk and Saris

130 **EARTH & WATER**
132 Tea and Cardamom
140 Working the Land
146 Fishermen

152 **THE PEOPLE**
154 Menswear
158 Women
162 School Kids

170 **SUNDAY AT THE BEACH**

174 **HOTEL RESOURCE GUIDE**

178 **ABOUT THE BOOK**
179 **ABOUT THE AUTHORS**

A member of the Thevar community from Thirumangalam, wearing a traditional gold earring. In Sanskrit, Thevar means celestial beings, divine natured-people.

FOREWORD

Shashi Tharoor

It is with pleasure that I welcome this beautiful addition to the short list of books about India that are both a delight to look at and instructive to read.

Melba Levick and Ameeta Nanji have seized south India whole – its art and its architecture, the quotidian sights and experiences of daily life, the ethos of a land both steeped in tradition and richly contemporary – and they have presented it in this wonderfully organized, sumptuous volume.

South India is the repository of much that is valuable in India's heritage, but it is much less well-known than the north. This book is an invaluable contribution to redressing this imbalance.

Workmen and women hand-washing the carved stone wall enclosure around Kailashnatha Temple, the oldest temple in Kanchipuram. The temple, dedicated to Shiva, was built in one of the earliest styles of Dravidian temple architecture between the late 7th century and early 8th century by the Pallava king, Raja Simha and his son.

ACKNOWLEDGEMENTS

This book could not have been possible without the most generous and professional assistance of Gita Bhalla of Equinox Travels in Delhi. For this we thank her and her colleagues, Meehak Prasad and Amit Shrivastava profusely.

We are grateful for the generous support of all the hotels who hosted us, listed in the Hotel Resource Guide, as well as to their gracious managers and staff.

Our deepest gratitude goes to Bela Khaleeli, Mallika Swaminadhan and Shamnad S.S. who gave us their time and expertise throughout our travels, making our trip all the more rich and interesting. Special thanks to Renjit for being such a safe driver.

Special thanks to Raj De Condappa at the beautiful Kailash Hotel in Pondicherry, Loulou Van Damme at Panchvatti in Goa and Meenakshi Meyyappan at The Bangala in Karaikudi for their hospitality and guidance. Thanks also to Francis Wacziarg of Neemrana Hotels for his continuous generosity and support; also to Jean Francois Lesage of the famous Vastrakala embroidery for making his extraordinary atelier in Chennai available to us for photographing. Through Shamnad S.S. we enjoyed the company of the following guides: Girija Duraiswamy, our guide in Mahabalipuram; Meenakshi Subramaniam, our guide in Karaikudi; S. Meenakshi, our guide in Madurai and Sujit Ranjan, our guide in Cochin.

For favours, large and small, we thank Lucinda Lester for her judicious 'eye', Mitchell Crites for his contacts and his support, Kathy Ho of Sheila Donnely Agency for her help with Taj Hotels, Sanjiv Vashist of Indiatourism Los Angeles for his assistance, and finally Meera Prashad and Kingfisher Airlines. Our appreciation as well to Kumarakom Lake Resort for allowing us to photograph their wonderful collections of instruments and architecture.

And last, but certainly not least, to the team at Roli Books, our persevering and wonderful editor, Priya Kapoor, our talented designer, Supriya Saran, and our terrific editor, Aditi Ghosh. We thank you for your brilliant work and your continuous patience.

INTRODUCTION

A priest holding objects used in daily puja. *Eleventh century Brihadisvarar Temple, Tanjore.*

Art and culture have always provided a bridge to mutual understanding amongst the peoples of the world – Anonymous

Civilization is the degree to which diversity is attained and unity is retained – W.H. Auden

Between the Malabar and Coromandal Coasts lie the Southern States of India, once collectively known as Dravida, from the Sanskrit word *drava*, water or sea. South India has the Arabian Sea to the west, the Bay of Bengal to the east and the Indian Ocean to the south. The estimated population of the area is 233 million. India is the second most populous country in the world, with over 1.8 billion people (as of April 2010). The larger linguistic groups in the south include the Telugus, Tamils, Kannadigas, Malayalis, Tuluvus, Kodavas and Konkanis. The states of Tamil Nadu, Kerala, Karnataka and Andhra Pradesh, the island of Lakshadweep and the territories of Pondicherry and tiny Goa, not only have their own languages and individual scripts, but also have their own ancient and contemporary literatures, their own newspapers, radio, TV programmes, films, art, music, dances and their own styles and flavours of clothing and cuisine.

It is a renowned fact that India has been dubbed the world's most multidimensional country. It can be divided into five regions – Northern, Southern, Eastern, Western and Central India. South India has its own vast share of unabashed diversity, from mist-shrouded mountains to sun-washed beaches, tranquil temples to feisty festivals, lantern-lit villages to hi-tech and software-supremo cities like Chennai, Bangalore and Hyderabad. The average literacy rate in South India is approximately 73 per cent, considerably higher than the Indian national average of 60 per cent. Kerala leads the nation with a literacy rate of 94.5 per cent.

Travelling by road, you see life in the countryside: Tamil Nadu and Kerala's fertile and green rice paddies edge the road, soothing the eyes and mind. Flowers smell sweet and are everywhere, *champa, frangipani, mogra*; whispering palms sway in the breeze along the coast and enormous spiky fruit dangle from the jack of all trees – the jackfruit tree.

Tumeric, star-anise, fennel, cinnamon sticks and dried ginger, speciality spices grown and cultivated in Cochin, Kerala.

Facing page: *Bananas being taken to market for sale in Madurai, Tamil Nadu.*

Then there are the *kaju* or cashew, the graceful and beautiful Areca (*Supari Palm*) and the feathery Tamarind (*Tamarindus Indica*) trees dotting the landscape.

Water is plentiful here, sourced by the Godaveri, Tungabhadra and Kaveri rivers. Two mountain ranges encompass this region, the Western and Eastern Ghats. The Nilgiris, or the blue hills, span Tamil Nadu and Kerala, so called because of a flower, *nilakurunji* or strobilanthus that blooms once every twelve years, covering the hills in shimmering shades of purple and blue.

Interspersed between countryside, villages, towns and big cities is a profusion of artistic creations, the splendid remnants of countless rulers' patronage and commitment to art, religion and power, in the form of innumerable edifices, from the Chera dynasty to the Pallavas, Chalukyas, Cholas and Pandyas and subsequently the Hoysalas and Nayakas. All left their mark in the form of exquisitely carved temple structures, great literatures, music, dance and more – testaments to the vision and refinement of these long-gone civilizations. This period extended from the fourth century BC until the seventeenth century AD, a span of over two thousand years.

Of all the elements that add to India's diversity, nothing has so enriched the land as its ancient philosophy. A common acknowledgement of, and respect for, a deeper presence exists everyday and everywhere. Hindu, Muslim, Christian, Jain, Parsi, Jew, Buddhist, Sikh - in India there really is no escape from religion. Art, ritual, religion, creativity and life are inseparable.

Every lake, river and mountain is a repository of some tale of divine mythology; every jungle is

FD
51
RRS.
RRS

marked with marigold flowers and a smear of red vermillion, showing where India's tribals have worshipped nature.

Trees feature often in Indian mythology, providing shade and sanctuary to the divine. The goddess Meenakshi resides in the forest at Madurai and the god Krishna's playground is always a sacred grove of trees. In Kanchi, Shiva appeared to a sage, sitting under a mango tree. That mango grove became a pilgrimage centre and all mango trees are since considered sacred.

Two-thousand-year-old sacred cities still flourish as pilgrims from all over the country come to the temples to worship. From Cochin to Chennai, merchant cultures still grow rich from her ancient ports, once part of the world's prosperous spice route extending from Java to Rome exporting black pepper, cardamom and nutmeg.

India is the sum of a million worlds, several civilizations in separate stages of development, co-existing despite their contradictions. The lack of homogeneity that has constantly been the challenge for rulers and governments in every age and so threatens today's assembly-line mentality is the essence of India's genius. Thank goodness for India's chaos. It is her greatest strength and a deep source for a living, stirring, thriving, colour-filled life. Nowhere is this more palpable than in the southern states of India.

Flower sellers wait for customers in Koyambedu Market, in Chennai, Tamil Nadu.

BACKWATER LIFE

Squat-looking houseboats of every size line the shores. Their concave upper decks and thatched roofs are made out of knotted coir fibres from coconut palm trees.

Whispering palm leaves reflect on the surface of the mirror-like water as you glide in a long wooden boat along the backwaters of Kerala. Flickering shadows and light play on the water's surface, creating a dreamy sensation of peaceful calm. All of a sudden a flash of turquoise breaks the calm as a kingfisher darts across the lagoon. Downstream, shimmering dragonflies hover over clusters of purple water hyacinths as you survey tranquil rural scenes: women washing clothes along the banks, barefoot children with satchels on their backs twittering cheerfully as they walk to school, men wearing *lungis* harvesting coconuts in the shaded palm groves.

The criss-cross network of canals bordered by acres of mangroves that covers Kerala is known as the backwaters. They have evolved a unique wetlands eco-system; freshwater from the rivers flowing down from the Western Ghats meets seawater from the Arabian Sea. Fresh water is

kept intact by the Thanneermukkon barrier on the Vembanad Kol (lake), one of the largest lakes in India, covering approximately 680 miles (1512 kilometres).

Besides supporting a wide array of flora and fauna, the wetlands and backwaters have provided a healthy livelihood and a wealth of resources to the communities living here. People along the backwaters are engaged in boat-building, fishing, sand-mining, coir making, limestone collection, rice farming and duck rearing. This has worked well as long as human activities and intervention have remained minimal. The mangroves act as natural filters and help remove a wide range of

Called kettuvalam *in Malayalam, these former rice barges around Mappuzha have been reincarnated as luxury floating palaces in the backwaters of Kerala.*

Facing page (top): *A family using a coracle to travel along the backwaters. Coracles have been around since the fifteenth century at least, and have changed little in their design. Woven with bamboo reeds and made waterproof with animal hide, they are light.*

Facing page (bottom left): *Literally meaning "boat tied together with rope",* kettuvalams *traditionally carried rice from the paddy fields before the advent of roads and improved transportation.*

Facing page (bottom right): *School children taking a break outside their classroom.*

A shady coconut palm grove. Although coconut trees grow along the Coromandal and Malabar coasts, Kerala grows more than half of India's total coconuts. The state's name derives from 'kera', coconut tree and 'alam' place of, making Kerala the 'land of coconuts'.

Facing page: *Endless reflections of gently swaying palms and lush vegetation create dreamy scenes all along the backwaters.*

pollutants from water, including harmful viruses from sewage and heavy metals from industries. Thus the ecosystem, through its all-encompassing balancing nature, was self-cleansing. Over the last decade things have been changing fast. All is not well in the backwaters. Pollution from unbridled industrial development, a population explosion and increased human activity has created an imbalance in this fragile ecosystem. Kerala's backwaters are disappearing and an environmental crisis is threatening the heart of one of the most beautiful corners of India. Life for the communities along the canals has always been hard and it gets more and more challenging every day. Fortunately these issues and problems are being examined by environmental and social organizations, which diligently seek solutions to restore balance to the backwaters and the wetlands surrounding them.

Backwater Cuisine

Kerala's long coastline, numerous rivers and backwater networks have contributed to India's rich fish and seafood cuisines. Coconuts are plentiful, especially along the backwaters and consequently, grated coconut and coconut milk are widely used in dishes and curries as a flavouring ingredient. Rice is grown in abundance, and could be said to be the main staple of the area. As with almost all Indian food, spices play an important part in the cuisine. The main spices used are cinnamon, cardamom, ginger, black peppers, green and red chillies, cloves, garlic, cumin seeds, coriander and turmeric.

A floating shop in Kumarakom: a local businessman carrying household wares to sell to communities living along the canals.

A woman washing clothes on the river banks. Water serves the purposes of trade and commerce, alongside daily chores in Kerala.

DEVOTION

Devotees surround and adorn a stone sculpture of Nandi at the Meenakshi Temple, Madurai, Tamil Nadu. In Hindu mythology, Nandi is the gate-keeper for Shiva and Parvati (represented here as Meenakshi). Temples venerating Shiva and Parvati display stone sculptures of a seated Nandi usually facing the main shrine.

Bhakti is translated as "devotion" to, or "participation" in a relationship usually with the divine. Devotion is perhaps the one thing that connects the people of India, transcending differences in languages, castes and religious beliefs. Devotion is expressed in myriad ways in every aspect of daily life, through religion, ritual and art.

Black granite sculpture of Nandi, measuring approximately twenty feet, facing the main shrine of Brihadisvarar Temple, Tanjore.

Hundreds of oil lamps being arranged for puja *at the Meenakshi Temple, Madurai.*

Meenakshi Temple, Madurai, Tamil Nadu.

Facing page (left): *Devotee at Chidambaram Temple.*

Facing page (right): *An elephant blessing a visitor at the entrance of the Brihadisvarar Temple, Tanjore. Elephants are revered in India as one of the* navratnas *(nine jewels) in Hindu mythology.*

A basket of fresh jasmine, lotus-buds and roses; fragrant offerings for the temple deities. Fresh flowers are offered to deities as a symbol of love and devotion.

Facing page: *Wide courtyards surround the various structures of the Brihadisvarar Temple, Tanjore, representing the zenith of the Chola dynasty under Emperor Rajaraja.*

A young lady drawing a kolam *with rice flour at the entrance of her home, near Kanchipuram. This spiritual activity is practiced by women in South India every morning.*

Facing page: Tikas *and* bindus *adorn a Lord Ganesha sculpture* (left), *a wandering* sadhu (top right)*and a householder* (bottom right). *The* sadhu's *hand and fingers are in* chin mudra. *The index finger represents the ego bowing to the thumb, representing the divine.*

SACRED MARKS

Kolams, Designs at the Threshold

Every morning at sunrise thousands of women in southern India draw kolams on the ground in front of their home. They are a sign of invitation to welcome all into the home, a daily tribute to harmonious co-existence. Kolams are the intricate geometrical patterns drawn by hand using powdered white rice. Throughout the day, the drawings get walked on, rained out, or blown around in the wind; new ones are made the next day.

Kolams are a testament to the skill and art of generations of women. Patterns are passed on from mother to daughter. They are an acknowledgement of the divine in everyday life, drawn with the intention of invoking good vibrations, auspicious thoughts and a sense of kindness to all living beings. The process of drawing a *kolam* is meditative, helping the woman focus her attention on creating something beautiful, and providing a pause, some quiet moments before the day's activities.

Bindu, Seed

Known by many names, *tilak, tilaka, tika*, bindi - it is the mark placed usually on the forehead between the eyebrows. Traditionally the mark, often a dot, symbolizes an invocation, a constant reminder of one's connection to divinity. The Sanskrit word *bindu* means seed. Metaphysically speaking, it is the dimensionless point of infinite potential from which all manifested existence originates. It is said to signify the mystical third eye and the channel of supreme wisdom and sublime intuition.

Tilaks made with sandalwood ash are smeared on the forehead and other parts of the body while a *bindu* is worn between the eyebrows. The powder used is called *kumkum* or *sindoor*, a mixture of powdered tumeric and a little bit of slaked lime which turns the yellow powder red. Married women apply *kumkum* in the parting of their hair as a symbol of marriage.

Shiva-shakti tilaks*: white symbolizes the masculine.*

Facing page (left): *The elephant is painted with an* 'om'*sign in Tamil* .

Facing page (right): *Red symbolizes the feminine aspects of divinity.*

A modern Bharatanatyam dance troupe performing in Chennai.

DANCE

Indian classical dance is a relatively new term for various codified art forms rooted in *Natya,* the sacred musical theatre styles. *Natya,* whose theory can be traced to the *Natya Shastra,* was compiled by the sage Bharata more than two thousand years ago. The text contains a set of precepts on the arts and while it primarily deals with stagecraft, it has influenced music, dance, sculpture, painting and literature. Throughout the centuries, dance has been a vehicle of worship and an expression of timeless universal human emotions. Modern dancers still dance according to the rules set forth in the *Natya Shastra.* Some of the best known classical dance forms have originated in South India: Bharatanatyam from Tamil Nadu, Kathakali, Theyyam and Mohiniattam from Kerala. Bharatanatyam, one of the oldest classical dance

A Kathakali dancer depicting Dhirodatta, the virtuous, noble-hearted hero. The green make-up known as pachcha *(green) is worn by the principled characters, who also wear an elaborately painted headgear called* kirita.

Facing page (left): *Theyyam dancer accompanied by a drummer playing the* chenda.

Facing page (right): *A young man performing a modern version of Bharatanatyam, the national dance of India.*

A group of dancers depicting wild animals practicing before their performance. Dance in South India is closely associated with divinity and spirituality.

forms, comes from the words *Bhava* (expression), Raga (music), *Tala* (rhythm) and *Natya* (drama).The most popular stories enacted in Kathakali are from the Mahabharata, about the "great stories", as pointed out by the Booker prize winning author, Arundhati Roy in The God of Small Things, 1997, "the ones you have heard over and over again. The ones you can enter anywhere and inhabit comfortably". Themes encompass the four goals of life: purpose, action, pleasure and liberation. Theyyam is a dance form from north-west Kerala traditionally performed by indigenous tribals of the region. People of these districts consider Theyyam divine and seek blessings from the dance and dancer. Mohiniattam literally means dance of the enchantress. The main theme of the dance is love and devotion for the divine, using feminine beauty to lure away ignorance from true knowledge. Each dance form is accompanied by its own particular music and vocals.

Kalaripayattu

They fly in the air, prowl low close to the earth and pulsate their limbs with ample dexterity, performing precise leg kicks and circling each others' bodies in complex gymnastic combinations. They are Kalaris, performing Kalaripayyatu, Kerala's traditional martial art. Kalaripayattu traces its roots as far back as the twelfth century when each village had its sacred training hall where both girls and boys became expert fighters under the eyes of a disciplined Kalari master.

The training hall consists of four walls surrounding a floor of earth, covered with a thatched palm-leaf roof. In one corner of the sacred training hall is housed the guardian deity on a tiered platform of seven steps representing the seven abilities a warrior must possess – strength, patience, discipline, grace, assertion, animal postures and wild animal sounds.

Kalaripayattu is one of the oldest existing martial arts of Indian origin. There are several styles of kalaripayattu depending on their regional origin. This northern style is distinguished by the emphasis on both physical training and the use of full-body massage. A medicinal oil massage increases flexibility and treats muscle injuries incurred during practice.

Two of the Pancha Rathas, *(Five Chariots) at Mahabalipuram, Tamil Nadu, built between the seventh and ninth centuries. The five monolithic pyramidal structures are named after the Pandavas (Arjuna, Bhima, Yudhishtra, Nakula and Sahadeva). An interesting aspect of the* rathas *is that despite their size, they are not assembled; each structure is carved from one single large piece of stone.*

THE TEMPLE

Dravidian architecture emerged as a style during the seventh century in southern India, drawing its structure from *Vastu Shastra*, the ancient treatise on the art and science of construction. It features pyramid-shaped temples, constructed with intricately-carved stone in a step design, and adorned with numerous statues of deities, warriors, demons and dancers. The statues depict legends from the great epics of Hindu literature and philosophy and continue to be a way these ancient stories remain alive and passed on from one generation to the next. South Indian kingdoms and empires, the Pallavas, Cholas, Pandyans, Cheras, Chalukyas, Rashtrakutas, Hoysalas, amongst many others, made a substantial contribution to the evolution of Dravidian architecture through the ages.

Dravidian-style temples consist almost invariably of four parts: *vimanam*, *mantapam*, *gopuram* and *chawadi*. The main part, the temple itself, is called *vimanam*. It is square in plan referring to the shape of a *mandala* (plan or chart) symbolically representing the cosmos. It is surmounted by a pyramidal roof of one or more stories and contains the shrine in which the image or symbol of the god or goddess is placed. The porches or *mantapams*, cover and precede the doorway leading to the main shrine.

Gate-pyramids, or *gopurams*, are the principal features in the quadrangular enclosures that surround the temples. Pillared halls, or *chawadis*, are used to house pilgrims during special occasions. Besides these architectural elements, a temple contains tanks or wells for water, dwellings for the priests and several other structures for state events.

A young visitor to a temple in Chidambaram, Tamil Nadu, watches a priest perform a religious ritual. In this manner, rituals are passed on from one generation to generation.

Facing page (left): *A flower seller displaying colourful garlands of* japa kusum *(yellow chrysanthemum and China rose hibiscus) outside the temple entrance at Tanjore.*

Facing page (right): *Pilgrims making their way through the main entrance to the Brihadisvarar Temple.*

Inside the Meenakshi temple in Madurai, hundreds of stalls throng the enormous structure of the temple as vendors sell their glittering wares to visitors: framed prints of goddess Meenakshi, sindoor *(vermillion powder), wall hangings, colourful beads, sacred threads in red, white and yellow and more.*

MEENAKSHI MADURAI

According to legend, the temple of Madurai is dedicated the warrior goddess Meenakshi, (of the fish-shaped eyes), avatar of Parvati and consort of Shiva, also known as Sundareshwarar (the beautiful one). She ruled the kingdom of Madurai skillfully. A Tamil poem describes Meenakshi as a woman washing pots and pans (which symbolize all the worlds). This is a daily task, because her husband Shiva repeatedly messes up the universe, which Meenakshi must once more sort out and clean. The union of Meenakshi and Sundareshwarar is a nightly ritual in Madurai, The priests of the temple, muscular shirtless men with lungis wrapped around their thighs, carry Shiva's palanquin on their shoulders. They march him slowly along a stone corridor shrouded in shadows, to his consort's shrine. Drumbeats echo along the

A naga *or snake shrine at the foot of a Neem tree in the main courtyard of the temple. Couples often hang clay figurines of baby Krishna in boxes as offerings so that they may be blessed with children.*

Facing page (left) *A newly painted section in the Meenakshi Temple with a brightly coloured stone sculpture of the Pallava's royal crest: Sinha, the Lion.*

Facing page (right): *One of the four* gopurams, *temple towers ornamented with a thousand brilliantly painted sculptures depicting a variety of mythological and auspicious themes.*

walls. Candles flicker outside the doorway to the shrine's inner sanctum. There, Meenakshi awaits the embrace of her husband, Sundareshwarar, an incarnation of that most priapic of Indian gods, Shiva.

The temple forms the heart and lifeline of the 2,500-year-old city of Madurai. Historical evidence reveals that the original temple was built approximately 2,000 years ago by the Pandyan king, Kulasekara, around which he created a lotus-shaped city. The Nayaks who ruled Madurai from the sixteenth to the eighteenth centuries continued its construction and created the majestic temple as it is today, a unique and spectacular example of Dravidian architecture.

Puja *offerings: tumeric root and* sindoor *sold loose for the temple or in little boxes for household use.*

Coconuts play a significant role in temple rituals. The hard shell symbolizes the ego; once this is broken, consciousness becomes as pure as the coconut flesh within.

WAY TO
SIVA TEMPLE

Priests light flames and chant mantras accompanied by drums, to ensure their night of conjugal bliss.

Left: *The nightly ritual of carrying Shiva into Meenakshi's shrine.*

ROADSIDE SHRINES

From left: *An array of roadside shrines, as simple as a stone; or tree, or carefully painted representations of gods and goddesses; a snake shrine atop a white-ant hill is dedicated to Mariamman, goddess of rain and protection from disease.*

Roadside shrines with their carefully placed objects of devotion smeared with red powder abound in southern India: in a rice paddy, under a tree, on a crowded pavement, on the side of a busy highway. It is common to see people, be they Muslim, Hindu or Christian, stop for a moment before a roadside shrine to fold their hands and offer short invocations to the gods. Dotted all over South India from Tamil Nadu to Goa, many roadside shrines are dedicated to regional and folk deities and are a common feature of worship.

A common sight in rural South India is an anthill, believed to be the resting place of snakes, guardians of the underworld. Snake worship is a combined animistic-Hindu form of worship and is particularly pronounced in South India. The early inhabitants,

like the present ones, had to face encounters with deadly snakes in forests and marshy grounds. They could think of no better way to console themselves from that fear than appeasement and veneration. Votive steles with snake images are often erected below trees and people offer milk and eggs to appease the snakes. In the countryside, shrines are created to guard fields, crops and herds and in gratitude for good weather and bountiful harvests.

Tree-shrines are also a frequent sight in India. Trees are often garlanded and festooned with scraps of colourful fabrics. A pilgrim on her journey or a passerby going about his daily life will see marks painted on a tree-trunk, or the image of a deity installed at the foot of the tree. No elaborate ritual is necessary; simply bowing down or throwing a flower connects the person with the divine.

Women offering prayers at a roadside naga *(snake) shrine.*

Left: *An unusual shrine of a reclining goddess, almost twenty feet long in Pondicherry.*

The grand central hall of a private residence owned by the M.S.M. Meyappan family, built in 1924. All family rituals, from birth to death, were held in this hall. The chandelier and other decorative details are from Europe, while the ceiling is a hand-tooled design on copper.

ARCHITECTURE & DESIGN

Indian architecture is the built expression of an interaction between a global culture and India's rich past, starting as far back as the flourishing Mehrgarh culture of the Indus Valley Civilization more than 5,000 years ago. This was followed by Hindu, Buddhist and Islamic traditions as well as village and tribal mud, brick, bamboo and thatch traditions, followed by the Portuguese, Danish, French and British colonial influence and the Art Deco movement. After Independence, the legacies and influence of Le Corbusier, Louis Kahn, and Charles Correa and other contemporary architects continue. Architects and designers are part of this rich cultural heritage of genius and beauty. These traditions remain a great source of inspiration, creativity and skill.

KARAIKUDI
KARAIKUDI

The hundred-year-old Chettinad Palace at Kanadukathan, Tamil Nadu, extends over 40,000 square feet. It is an outstanding example of Chettinad architecture. The oldest surviving building of this style, the Chettinad Palace was built by S.A. Ramaswamy Chettiar in 1902.

CHETTINAD STYLE

Neo-classical, Art Deco, Victorian, intricate Kerala woodwork, Mandalay, Anglo-Indian, Tamil - all these styles and colours in one mansion clash, collide and unexpectedly create a grandiose, whimsical style all of its own – Chettinad, a style that speaks loudly and clearly of a time of prosperity, grandeur and artistic opulence. The mansions feature numerous styles of pillars made of teak, and sometimes, iron. High ceilings, marble floors, elaborate grill work on balconies and staircases are some of other the main features. They are particularly known for their silky-smooth, specially plastered walls which remain cool to the touch even in the hottest of summers.

The mansions were built on rectangular plots. They are so vast that most of them stretch between two streets, the front door opening into one street

and the back into the next. If you were to enter a Chettinad house, the architectural design compels your gaze along a straight line from the huge front door, through a series of inner courtyards, ending at the much smaller back door.

Chettinad, a region in the south-east of Tamil Nadu, is the homeland of the Nattukottai Chettiars, a prosperous banking and business community, many of whom migrated to Ceylon and Burma in the nineteenth and early twentieth centuries. They shipped home Burmese teakwood, Italian marble, Spanish tiles, English steel, Belgian mirrors and chandeliers amongst other materials to build and decorate their mansions. The Chettiar's main intent was to make his house a statement of his social success and he put everything into it, borrowing details from European and Asian architecture styles, seen during his travels abroad.

An etched glass mirror imported from Belgium hangs majestically in the hall of MSMM House. It is used by the Meyappan family for celebrating weddings, birthdays and religious festivals.

Facing page*: Reception area in a Chettiar home.*

Following pages (left): *A long pillared corridor joins different parts of Visalam Mansion, which has been converted into a museum. It contains valuable furniture, household utensils and traditional Chettiar textiles.*

Following pages (centre): *Chettiar mansions rival the* havelis *(courtyard homes) of Shekavati in Rajasthan. However, unlike the* havelis *whose walls are painted with murals, the Chettiars used patterned porcelain tiles imported from Belgium to decorate their walls.*

Following pages (right): *An ornate painted iron spiral staircase tucked into the corner of Chettiar Palace.*

HEARTY WELCOME TO YOUR EXCELLENCIES

Architectural details from Chettiar Palace; the intricate grill work (top) *and the multicoloured stained glass* (bottom).

Facing page: *The magnificent entrance of the Chettiar Palace in Karaikudi, Tamil Nadu, was built by S.A.R. Ramaswamy Chettiar in 1902.*

An exquisitely hand-carved Burmese teak pillar displaying the great workmanship that went into these mansions.

Facing page: *Several families are returning to their ancestral homes with renewed pride, determined to restore them and appreciate the skills that went into these buildings.*

Following pages: *A traditional Kerala home, known as* Nalukettu, *that has been transformed into a holiday dwelling. The roofs are tiled or thatched with palmyrah and coconut leaves and project out at several layers in order to protect the inner skeletal framework from the vigorous monsoons that often flood this region.*

DWELLINGS

Goan-Portuguese villas. The Portuguese colonized Goa for four centuries, and influenced the architectural style as can be seen in many buildings.

A distinctive Goan architectural feature is the front portico supported by two pillars. It provides a cool seating area for siestas, especially during the hot summer months.

Rural construction techniques to build a hut use mud for walls and floors, bamboo for trellis work, Casuarina and palm leaves for thatched roofs, all found locally throughout Tamil Nadu.

A house on the outskirts of Cuddalore, Tamil Nadu. Today, architects are revisiting these constructions since they are cost effective and suited to the climate, enabling the integration of conventional and modern materials for rural construction.

DETAILS

Clockwise: *Architectural and ornamental details found in traditional Kerala homes; an ancient metal padlock; functional carved metal details decorating a wood door; solid wood beams and bannister provide support to a ceiling; a small hand carved painted wood panel of the goddess Lakshmi set into a larger panelled wall.*

A spacious verandah with Indo-Portuguese colonial furniture, overlooking lush gardens in Panchvatti, Goa in the island of Corjeum.

LIVING SOUTH

A serene courtyard shaded by trees in the French Quarter, Pondicherry.

Bottom: *A view of the verandah at Panchvatti where there are many places to sit and dream.*

A beautiful and soothing courtyard viewed through arches, Pondicherry.

Bottom*: Indo-Portuguese furniture at Le Colonial, a restored sixteenth-century mansion in Fort Cochin. It now serves as a resorted luxury boutique hotel.*

Flowers are skillfully arranged in an uruli.

Facing page: *A variety of flower designs made by carefully placing flowers in an* uruli *(metal vessel), so that they float on the water. Used as cooking vessels, they can still be found in traditional Kerala kitchens.*

Fanciful Facades

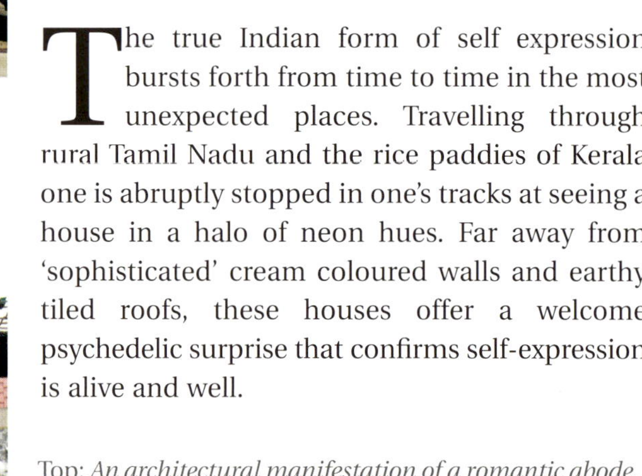

The true Indian form of self expression bursts forth from time to time in the most unexpected places. Travelling through rural Tamil Nadu and the rice paddies of Kerala one is abruptly stopped in one's tracks at seeing a house in a halo of neon hues. Far away from 'sophisticated' cream coloured walls and earthy tiled roofs, these houses offer a welcome psychedelic surprise that confirms self-expression is alive and well.

Top: *An architectural manifestation of a romantic abode.*

Bottom: *This cinema house in Cuddalore, Tamil Nadu, is now a kitsch classic; its architectural style being influenced by the design of a sixteen-millimetre movie camera.*

Facing page: *In Tamil Nadu, there is a trend of houses being painted in bright colours. It is commonly believed that certain colours are lucky and bring good fortune.*

Raja.v...

THE STREET

An elderly lady selling lotus flowers outside a temple in Pondicherry.
One of the most ancient symbols in India, the lotus flower represents purity of heart and mind as it remains untouched by the muddy waters from which it is born.

India's streets are truly a melting pot of her culture. People take to the streets on all important festive occasions, whether they are celebrating a wedding, a victory or a religious event. The street is a marketplace where people sell their wares and, indeed, for a large number of people, the streets are the stage where the drama of their entire life unfolds.

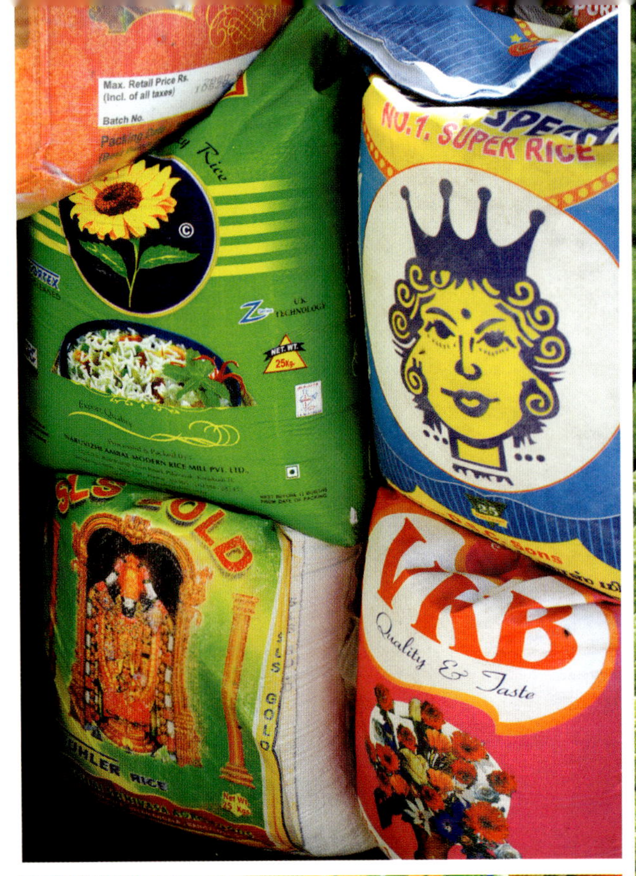

Max. Retail Price Rs.
(Incl. of all taxes)
Batch No.
NO.1. SUPER RICE
VRB
Quality & Taste
SLS GOLD

88

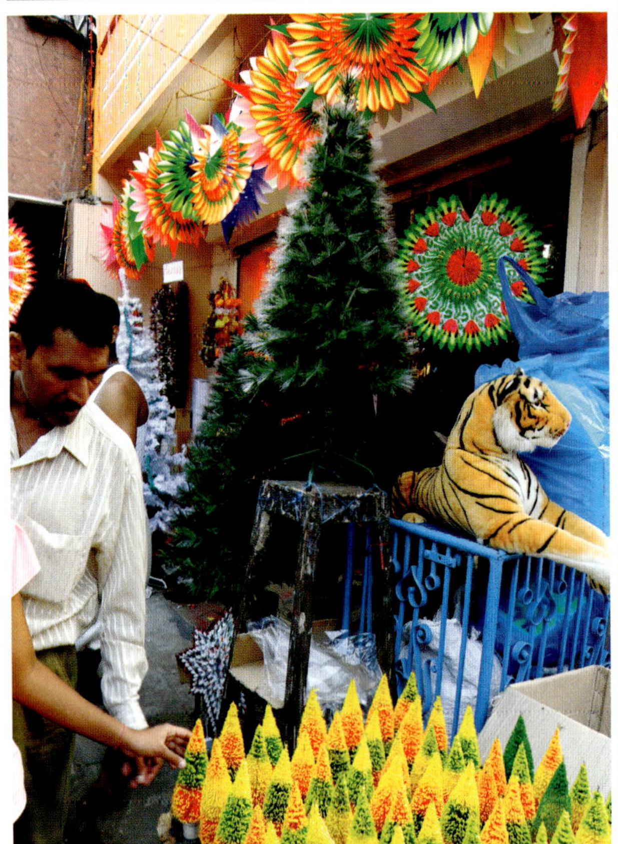

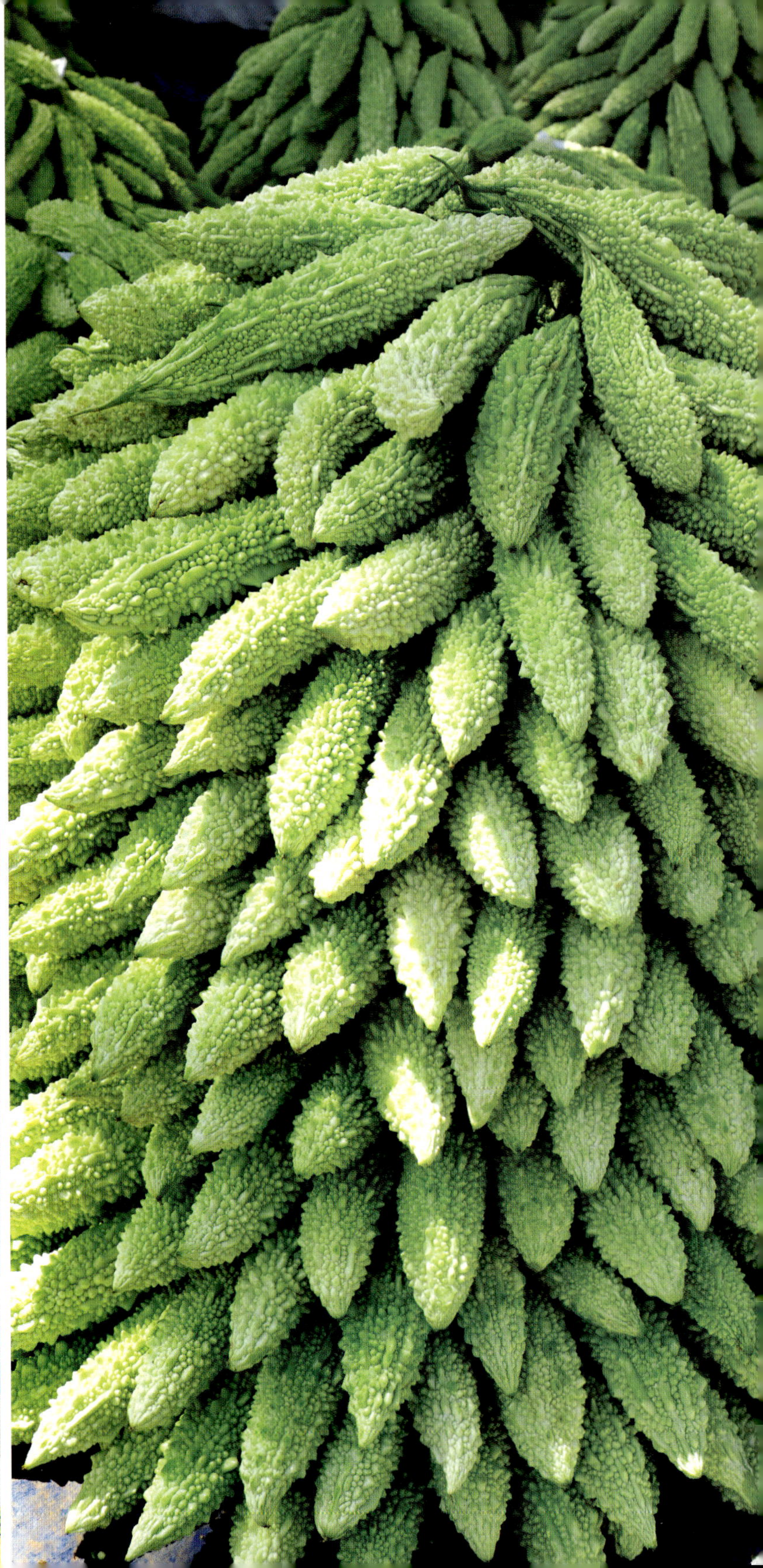

Bazaars

Bustling bazaars attract everyone. They have enticed traders and buyers for millennia as ideas and culture were exchanged along with goods. Sea and land routes developed with the silk and spice trades that had their beginnings in street bazaars. Spices and textiles were traded with the West in exchange for wine, olive oil and Roman coins.

Today, as in the past, certain streets are dedicated to special items; fabrics and clothes, herbs and spices, decorations for festivals, hand-made papers, fruit, flowers and vegetables, jewellery and gold. The Great Indian Bazaars offers something to everyone and many items are still crafted by hand by traditional artisans. Bazaars continue to attract people from everywhere and are the best place to mingle with the locals, find locally-grown produce and products made in the area.

Far left (top): *Striking graphics on bags of rice and flour stacked for sale.*

Far left (bottom)*: Christmas trinkets on the streets of a Cochin bazaar.*

Centre and right: *A vegetable and produce market in Madurai where women vendors sell* pudalangai *(snake-gourd),* pagarkai, *(bitter melon), green chillies and onions.*

PILES
Dr. DAS
PILES
Dr. DAS

Festive decorations hanging, ready for sale during Christmas in the Jew Market at Cochin. The most famous Jew Market in Kerala is located at Ernakulam.

Mobile street vendors selling shiny stainless steel pots, tiffins, cooking utensils and an array of food containers. They are a common sight in the streets of South Indian towns.

The idea of stacking and storing containers comes from earlier times when women carried stacked pots on their heads; many still do today.

A wooden masala dabba *(spice box) containing various spices, including dried red chillies, nutmeg, fennel, star aniseed, cloves, black pepper and mustard seeds.*

STREET FOOD & SPICES

No country in the world grows as many varieties of spices as India, and the southern states, especially Kerala, are known to be one of the largest spice producers. Tamil Nadu, Karnataka and Andhra Pradesh are well known for their cultivation of paprika and a wide variety of chilli. Cochin continues to be a major trade centre of spices, famous for its black pepper, cloves, ginger and nutmeg. In ancient times, spices were as precious as gold and crucial as medicines, preservatives and perfumes. The history of Indian spices can be traced to 7,000 years ago. It is a chequered history, of lands discovered and destroyed, kingdoms built and brought down, wars won and lost. Historical evidence tells us in 80 BC, when the Egyptian city of Alexandria became the busiest commercial centre on earth,

From top left: *Sugar-cane juice is popular as a thirst quencher in the hot climate and provides the benefits and energy of pure sucrose, which are lost when it is processed into white sugar; a menu outside a roadside toddy bar in Kerala, serving shrimp curries and other delicacies, eaten with palm wine; a toddy bar in Kerala. In many villages of South India, palm toddy is a common drink. Known in Andhra as* karloo, *this white fizzy alcoholic drink is made from the sap of the Palmyra;* sadya, *a traditional banana leaf thali from Kerala, contains an array of different curries and includes rice, pappadam,* rasam *(spicy pepper water) grilled fish and prawns; a Bombay* paanwallah *in Munnar preparing* paan *(betel leaf). Now known as Mumbai, Bombay is renowned for its specialty* paans.

its bazaars were stocked with Indian spices en route to markets in Greece and the Roman Empire. Sailing ships were carrying Indian spices, perfumes and textiles to Mesopotamia, Arabia and Egypt. It was the lure of these exotic products that brought many seafarers to the shores of India.

Street food in India is an amalgamation of mouth-watering flavors and spices that stimulate the taste buds. Each Indian city specializes in its own variety of street food. In the southern states street corners are dotted with food stalls doling out hot *idlis*, *medu vadas*, *uthappams*, or spreading a *thattu dosa*, or *thalluvandi* on a hot griddle, all served with traditional *sambar* and coconut *chutney*.

Beverages are no exception. Apart from the manufactured aerated drinks, you can have a glass of lassi with the thickness and the froth of your choice. There are all kinds of tea – lemon tea without milk or sugar, green tea, masala tea, mint tea, milk-tea and normal tea. You can have hot milk served in a conical earthen pot called a *kulhad* or you may choose one of the many fruit juices and milk shakes on the menu of a juice stall. A favourite in the hot sweltering heat of summer is tender coconut and sugar-cane juice spiced up with a dash of lemon and a little ginger juice.

Although *paan* refers to the leaves of the betel vine, the common use of the word refers to the chewing mixture wrapped in betel leaves. There are hundreds of varieties of *paan*. The usual mixture inside a sweet paan includes paper thin slices of dry areca nut, sweet syrup and fennel seeds. *Paan* is usually eaten after a meal to assist digestion and act as a breath freshener.

An array of street food sold along the roadside, including fresh cucumbers, (left) *coconuts,* (centre) *boiled peanuts and hot* masala chai(right).

Flower sellers at Koyambedu Malar Angadi, the Chennai Flower Market.

FLOWERS

Inside a labyrinthine network of dark alleyways lit by electric bulbs is Koyambedu Malar Angadi, the Chennai Flower Market. This sprawling cement structure the size of a good-sized southern Tamil temple is the main supply-point of the huge flower trade. Large garlands of red roses and white tube-roses, shaped like cobras, hang on pillars on the outer-most stalls, while several pathways lead into cooler interiors.

During flower-traffic, crowds of people stepping cautiously on discarded fallen flowers that carpet the stone floors move from one seller to the next to get the best price. A thick scent of flowers and humidity hangs in the air as diligent sellers gracefully sprinkle water on their fragile wares. Customers at this wholesale market are almost as diverse as the flowers – ranging from pavement

An intricately woven garland next to a pile of malligai *(jasmine buds), commonly worn by women in their hair.*

flower sellers or small florists to large exporters who buy and sell flowers nationally and internationally.

Flowers play an important role in people's daily lives. Women usually wear flowers in their hair. People and idols are garlanded as a sign of respect, devotion and welcome. Ancient literature and philosophy are full of the names of a variety of flowers. Certain flowers are linked with specific gods and goddesses. Lakshmi, the goddess of abundance, is usually depicted seated on a flowering lotus, while Krishna is often depicted as a Kadamba tree (*Anthocephalus indicus*).

Flower vendors making garlands and showing their colourful and fragrant wares outside Koyambedu market. Karnataka and Andhra Pradesh are major flower growing South Indian states, mainly exporting flowers to the United States of America, the Netherlands, Germany and Great Britain.

Flower decorations on the bride's hair; the groom looks on with pride.

Facing page: *Flowers in the hair give a distinct elegance to everyday life.*

A cut-out of M.K. Alagiri, politician and son of M. Karunanidhi, the Chief Minister of Tamil Nadu.

Facing page*: Larger than life, a kitsch statue at a village en route Auroville from Pondicherry, of M.G. Ramachandra, a matinee idol-cum-politician, in his trademark fur cap and dark glasses.*

Following pages: *The use of graffiti, known locally as 'wall writing'* (top centre), *banners, posters* (bottom centre) *and colourful plywood cut-outs of politicians* (top left), *deities* (far right) *and film stars* (bottom left) *create a vibrant and lively street scene in Tamil Nadu.*

BANNERS & CUTOUTS

No other state in India is as film-struck as Tamil Nadu. Here film idols turned politicians are worshipped as deities. Heroes and heroines are represented by gigantic cut-outs and posters. They used to worship M.G. Ramachandran, Sivaji Ganesan and Jayalalitha and now they worship M. Karunanidhi and his son Alagiri who are powerful politicians today. There was a time when whichever way you turned in Tamil Nadu you would see enormous cut-outs of the living gods doing namaskaram to you. However, over the past decade, hand-painted posters and cut-outs are becoming a thing of the past. They are an example of a slowly dying industry of mass communication being overtaken by electronic printing processes. Regional governments have banned the use of public space for political views. Ironically this ban also prevents the public from airing their views.

எங்கள்
சுவாசமே
கோ.தளபதி
N.சுரேஷ்பாபு
ரா.கண்ணன்
P.பொன்ராஜ்

மணி
மார்ட்

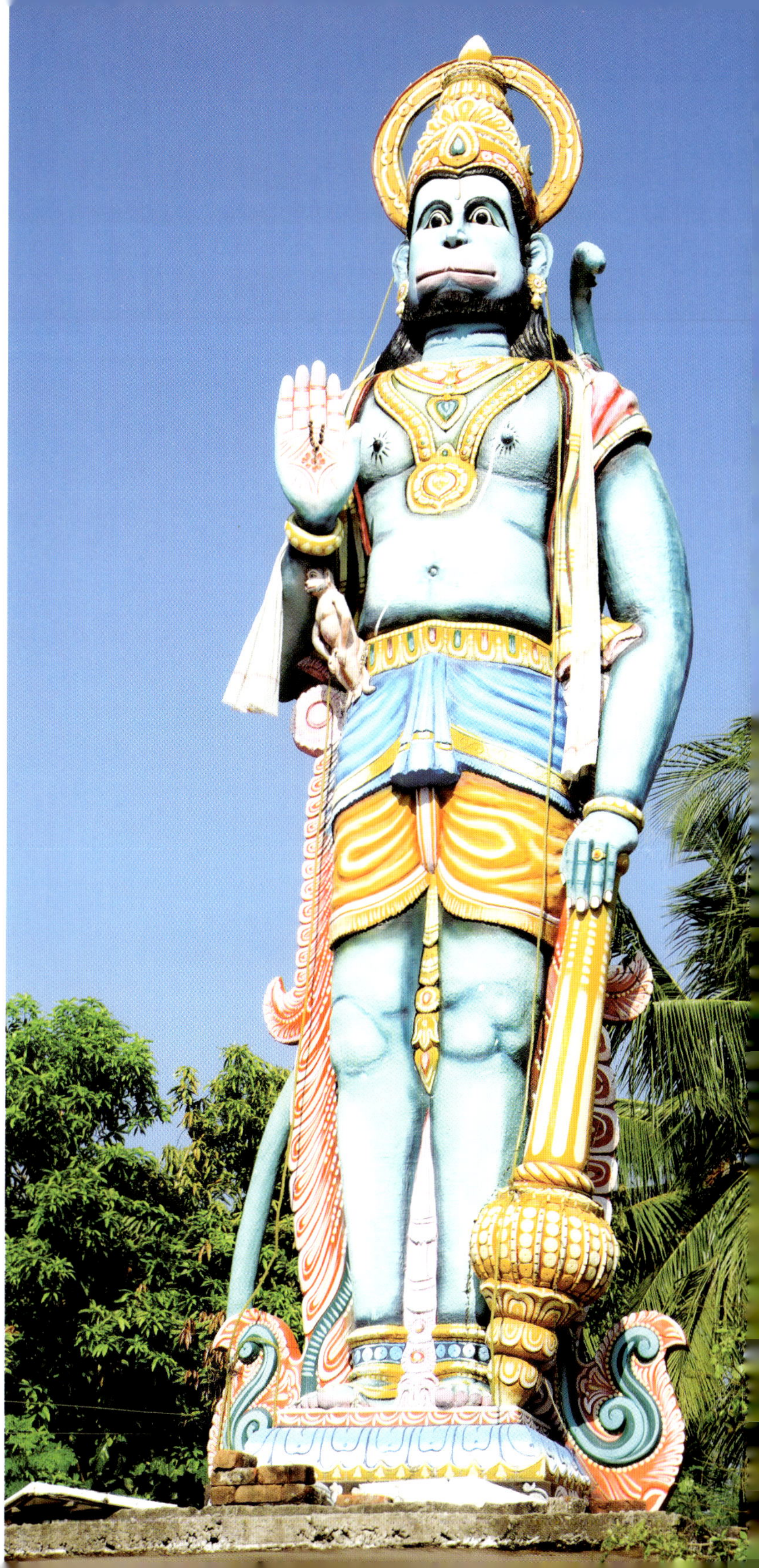

*A man weaving a coiled bamboo cane basket in his village near Cochin. Weaving baskets is an art as ancient as pottery in India. Until recently, whole families and entire villages were involved in bamboo-weaving. For hundreds of years, Dalit and Adivasi communities (Parayas, Pulayas, Kuravas, Mavilas and Vetuvas) of Kerala have transformed bamboo reeds (*Ochlandra travancorica*) into a variety of functional objects. Their creativity and skill in adapting to continually changing needs have seen the weavers making a wide range of items including baskets, beautiful mats, winnowers, window screens and many bamboo products for use in agriculture and fisheries.*

In India craftspeople have demonstrated a thorough understanding of materials combined with a mastery of tools, techniques, skill and creativity that have evolved over the centuries through social and cultural interactions. Handmade objects have their roots in function: things required for daily living from the mundane to the sacred. This has connected people to a greater tradition. However for many craftspeople, life has not been easy. Over the years handmade objects and craftspeople have been marginalized as a result of mechanization and mass production. Yet it is common to meet empowered, charismatic, innovative women and men working their traditional crafts, in all corners of the country, who against all odds live creative lives with dignity, grace and imagination. More recently there has been a large and important revival of handmade crafts especially due to organizations that recognize their value and of the oral knowledge systems that support them. The conservation and promotion of crafts and their makers is seen as a significant social, cultural, and economic force.

HANDWORK

S. Dhenalpal, a master vina *maker in Tanjore. Vinas are made from the jackfruit tree, which grows locally especially in Panruti, Tamil Nadu. It is a tree in the mulberry family. Jackfruit wood is also used to make the* mridangam *(drum), and* kanjira *(a frame drum of the tambourine family).*

Facing page (left): *A young boy hand carves a stone lion in Mahabalipuram.*

Facing page (right)*: A young man tying strips of bamboo together to make a window screen. The string is weighed down by stones keeping the screen and string in place.*

The process of basket weaving; an art in itself.

Facing page: *Nimble hands at work create an embroidered fabric, stitch by stitch in Vastrakala, Chennai.*

A skilled potter setting the wheel in motion with the help of a tall stick.

Facing page (left and right): *He then dampens the clay and skillyfully centres it to shapes it into a pot.*

Coir reels ready for weaving. Mats and baskets made of coir are very common in several households.

COCONUT & COIR

In Sanskrit, the name for the coconut palm, *kalpa vriksha,* means the tree which provides all the necessities of life. Palm trees belong to one of the world's oldest plant families and it is believed that coconut palms have been cultivated for at least 4,000 years. Coconut palms flower monthly and yield fifty to two hundred coconuts per year. The most commonly held view is that coconuts originated around the Pacific Islands and were distributed on ocean currents, cultivating themselves on warm, tropical shores around the world.

Within the smooth green outer shell is a fibrous husk eventually made into coir. The tree draws in water, whether saline or muddy, and transforms it into nutritious coconut water. The white flesh within (known as *copra*) and the coconut water together form the edible endosperm. The hard shell

A skilled worker weaving a coir mat on a handloom.

Right: *Equipped with his traditional tools, an expert palm tree climber trims palm fronds.*

Facing page: *Women coir workers walk backwards to spin long strands of yarn from the coir fibres held in their aprons. Two strands are intertwined for strength.*

of the seed or endocarp is used to make containers. As the seed matures, the liquid turns into a solid, pure white endosperm, rich in triglyceride oils. This is eaten widely and used in rituals. The solid endosperm, is also often dried and pressed to release the oil widely used in shampoos, soaps, moisturizing creams and butters. Palm wine, called toddy is the sap collected from the flowers of the palm tree. The sap is extracted and collected by a tapper who fastens a container around the flowers atop the palm tree.

Coir, from the Malayali word *kayar*, meaning cord, is made from the rich, coarse fibre extracted from the husk of the coconut. Bio-degradable, resistant to abrasion, durable and water-resistant with natural shock-absorbing qualities, coir's strength and coarse texture is perfect for a wide range of uses; it is made into brushes, sacks, rugs and rope and often blended with other natural fibres. Coir is the only natural fibre resistant to salt water, making it ideal for make nets and rope meant for marine use.

SILK & SARIS

A folktale explains the origin of the sari as follows: the sari, it is said, was born on the loom of a fanciful weaver. He dreamt of a woman. The shimmer of her tears. The drape of her tumbling hair. The colours of her many moods. The softness of her touch. All these he wove together. He couldn't stop. He wove for many yards. And when he was done, the story goes, he sat back and smiled and smiled and smiled.

Most saris are a woven as a single piece of cloth but the two-piece sari, *mundum neriyathum* or *set-mundu,* is traditionally worn by women in Kerala. It is a set of two *mundus* (woven fabric), both having matching borders. The set contains a lower and upper garment. The upper *mundu*, worn with a *choli* (fitted blouse), is wrapped once around the waist and upper body and placed over the left

Devotees pay homage to Shiva in his form as Nataraja, the lord of the dance at Brihadisvarar temple in Tanjore. They are wearing traditional Kerala Kasavu saris typically worn for special occasions.

Facing page: *A skein of silk threads are first put into a solution of water and citric acid to drench the silk fibres, then immersed in a blue dye solution. The amounts of dye are based on the weight of the yarns. The dyer moves the skein in an up -and-down motion in and out of the dye-bowl, which is heated by a flame. The yarns are then left to simmer as they absorb the dye .*

Drying silk threads in the sunlight near Vandiyur Mariamman Teppakulam, an island pavilion a few kilometres from the Meenakshi temple in Madurai.

Centre: *Weaving a silk sari in Kanchipuram using a handloom. Due to their double warp and double weft, silk Kanchipuram saris are amongst the most valued silks in the world. The gold in the motifs is incorporated by dipping the silk thread into liquid gold and silver.*

shoulder, resembling a sari's pallu, while the lower is tied around the waist, to cover the legs. They are made of unbleached cotton woven with a gold border on each edge of the sari, called *kasavu* or *kara*.

The wide variety of traditional saris from South India include Chettinad saris, Gadwal saris, Kanchipuram (also known as Kanjivaram) saris, Konrad saris, Mysore silk saris and Pochampally saris, each named after the region they come from. Each one is recognized for its particular design elements and colours.

Kanchipuram in Tamil Nadu, the City of Gold, is renowned for its distinctive weaving style. The tradition of silk-sari weaving here arose out of temple traditions from at least four hundred years ago. Primarily a temple town with over a hundred temples, Kanchipuram was the location for many festive and religious occasions. Spectacular saris were required by the maharanis, nobility and other affluent women attending these impressive events. It is often said that a woman's sari collection is incomplete without a Kanchipuram sari.

An emporium in Kanchipuram displaying a shimmering array of exquisitely hand-woven silk saris. One feels a thrilling surge of surprise, as piece by piece unfurls, revealing detailed ornate craftsmanship.

Above: *A vibrant mosaic of saris. Large and small* bootis, *buds, in gold and silver dispersed against the dark background shine like stars on a night sky. The Chettinad cotton sari is unique in the dramatic use of colour and pattern with bold checks, stripes and contrasting traditional hues; maroon, peacock blue, parrot green, mango yellow and vermillion red.*

Below: *Skeins of dyed silk threads ready to be woven into saris.*

Facing page: *A lady weaving a handloom cotton sari in Karaikudi.*

EARTH & WATER

A sea of emerald green. A paddy field is a flooded piece of arable land used for growing rice and is usually found near rivers and marshes. Flooding provides water essential for growing the rice crop. Paddy is cultivated at least twice a year, the two seasons are known as rabi *and* kharif. Rabi *cultivation is dependent on irrigation, while* kharif *largely depends on the monsoon rains.*

Approximately half of the population of South India is involved in agriculture, which is largely dependent on seasonal monsoons. During the monsoons, the country is usually blessed with generous rains. However, this bountiful monsoon can turn into disaster, causing uncontrollable floods in parts of the country. Every few years, the monsoon can be erratic and scarce, leading to drought and the possibility of famine.

Some of the main crops cultivated in South India are rice, sorghum, pearl millet, pulses, sugarcane, cotton, chilli, and ragi. Areca nut, coffee, tea, vanilla, rubber, pepper, tapioca, and cardamom are cultivated on the hills, while coconut grows abundantly in coastal areas. Andhra Pradesh is the largest producer of rice in India and Karnataka produces more than half of India's coffee.

Plantation workers wear large burlap bags on their back and thick plastic aprons. They move among the tea plants, briskly plucking tea. The tea plant is a single-stem bushy plant ranging from twenty to sixty centimeters in height.

TEA & CARDAMOM

The Ghats greet you like a breath of fresh air. The cool mountain tops are shrouded in mist. There are narrow winding lanes, waterfalls and sprawling tea plantations with ochre pathways. Red corrugated roofs dot the endless green hills.

Here lies Munnar, a tea town tucked into the the mountain ranges, and strategically located at the confluence of the Muthirappuzha, Nallathani and Kundaly rivers. Until the middle of the nineteenth century, these mountain jungles were the domain of tribal hunters and gatherers. Before the land was cleared for planting tea Munnar was essentially a rainforest and one can still discover areas where the jungles are teeming with insects, snakes and birds, amid soaring canopies of trees, plants and exotic flowers. Besides growing tea, Munnar cultivates many varieties of spices like cinnamon, cloves, peppercorns, nutmeg and cardamom.

The rolling hills are fastidiously adorned with tea plants, lush tiles that stretch to the horizon. The plantations are relentlessly manicured; the perfect fields of green reflect the elegance of high tea. And while the vistas are endless, the beauty is finite, overcome with tales of an eerie colonial past.

According to historical research, tea *(Camellia sinensis)*, locally called chai, has been known for millennia as a medicinal plant and the consumption of tea is documented in the ancient epic Ramayana.

British settlers planted the first tea in Munnar in 1880. As part of a nascent network of trade, the commodity turned hallmark item had to compete with other producers globally. This financial push demanded monoculture farming on an unprecedented scale, a model that conflicted with local farmers then and continues to haunt this dwindling sector today. Today, Kanan Devan owns 80 per cent of the tea fields in Munnar and offers a long list of benefits to its workers while paying a salary of 118 rupees a day, (approximately 3 US dollars) for working eight to nine hours. And while the wafting aromas of cardamom and ginger linger, the strife of tea pickers and farmers, both those toiling on industrial plantations and those fighting to save family farms, stirs curiosity. Questions to

Top left: *Harvesting cardamom in the rainforests of Munnar. The cardamom bush grows to a height of about six feet and needs indirect sunlight.*

Bottom left: *Tea pickers start walking early in the morning along the streets of Munnar to reach the plantations.*

Facing page (top): *A group of young women enjoy a cup of tea.*

Facing page (bottom left): *Cardamom grows best in a warm, humid climate with rich, loamy soil.*

Facing page (bottom right): *Tea pickers before starting their day's work.*

ponder - Where does our tea come from? Who is producing it and at what cost?

Cardamom is popularly known as *elaichi* or *elchi*; *elakkai* in Malayalam and *yelakki* in Kannada.It is a tropical fruit of the ginger family, Zingiberaceae and comes in two forms, Elettaria and Amomum. Both varieties take the form of a small seedpod, with a thin, outer shell and small black seeds. Elettaria pods are light green, while Amomum pods are larger and dark brown. Cardamom plants grow wild in parts of the Western Ghats known as the Cardamom Hills. The warm humid climate, loamy soil rich in organic matter, monsoon rain, special cultivation and processing methods all combine to make the delicate green Malabar cardamom unique in aroma.

The Greeks started importing cardamom, known as the Queen of Spices, as a digestive medicinal herb. It was one of the most popular oriental spices in Roman cuisine and substantial quantities came from South India as early as the first century AD. Cardamom also has a long history as a medicine and as a herb to flavour food and drinks. The *Charak Samhita,* a medicinal text written between the second century BC and the

Most tea harvesting is done by women who have acquired the skill through years of experience, harvesting only the tenderest leaves.

Facing page (top): *The unripe ovoid shaped fruit of the cardamom plant.*

Facing page (bottom left): *An experienced tea picker can pluck up to thirty kilos of tea leaves in a day.*

Facing page (bottom right): *After a hard day's work on the plantations, tea workers prepare to have their tea collection weighed.*

second century AD mentions cardamom as a key ingredient in the preparation of medicines for curing a range of ailments.

In the eleventh century, cardamom was included in the list of ingredients for *panchasugandha-thambula* or 'five-fragrance betel chew' It was also included in recipes from the court of the Sultan of Mandu in the 1500s. These recipes included sherbets and rice flavoured with cardamom. Today cardamom continues to be a key ingredient in mithai, (Indian sweets) *chai* and *garam masala.*

Panoramic views of mist filled valleys and verdant tea plantations surround the tea town of Munnar, Kerala.

Above*: An early morning cardamom harvest. The bush begins to bear fruit after several years and is harvested every thirty days.*

WORKING THE LAND

Oxen are still commonly used to plough muddy paddy fields in Kerala. A plough consists of a wooden plank to tie the oxen and an iron bar attached to the plank, that tills the land. The plough helps to bring the low-lying soil to the upper layer and move the top layer to the bottom, aerating the ground. Oxen continue to be the mainstay of theagricultural system due to India's large rural economy. Particularly in South India, the ox is the village farmer's combination of a tractor, thresher and family car, as they are also used for transporting goods and people to and from towns.

Women plant seedlings by hand in rows in puddled fields.

Facing page (left): *A bundle of tender rice saplings ready to be planted.*

Facing page (right): *Throughout the growing period, water levels in the paddy fields are kept a few inches deep to prevent weeds and to ensure there is enough water for the plants to grow. This is done by irrigation or by the monsoon floods.*

Brick making in Chengalpattu, Tamil Nadu. Brick-making work has changed little since ancient times.

Facing page (top and bottom): *In the brick kilns of Tamil Nadu, life for the workers and their families is hard. In the absence of economic opportunities where they live, many migrate across the states of India to seek casual employment. Brick production depends almost entirely on migrant workers, half of whom are women.*

Fishermen returning after a night of fishing at Mahabalipuram, Tamil Nadu.

FISHERMEN

Scenes along the Coromandal and Malabar coasts. Though the towns and villages along the southern coasts of India have developed a thriving tourist industry in recent years, many of their economies have always been based on fishing

Facing page (top): *In the wake of the 2004 tsunami, many fishermen and women living in the lower areas along the coast found themselves without boats, nets or homes.*

Facing page (bottom left and right): *Today, with the help of various social organizations, the fishing boats are once more prowling the Bay of Bengal, restoring fisherfolk to their former livelihood.*

Regina
படவேட்ட அம்மன்

Women waiting on the beach to buy freshly caught fish directly from the fishermen to sell in the local market in the outskirts of Pondicherry.

Facing page: *These fishing nets are huge mechanical contrivances that hold out horizontal nets. Each structure comprises a cantilever with an outstretched net suspended over the sea and large stones suspended from ropes as counterweights at the other end.*

THE PEOPLE

Lungis *are worn for work; here, devotees are wearing traditional* lungis *at a stall outside a temple in Pondicherry.*

Previous pages (from left): *A silk dyer in Kanchipuram, holding skeins of thread before they are sent to be dried in the sun; a lady preparing banana leaves to sell at the market, where they are used to wrap temple offerings and serve as thalis for food; the foreman of a cardamom grove.*

MENSWEAR

The *lungi* originated in South India, and remains the traditional clothing for men in this region until today. It is available in a single colour, or with checks, prints and stripes and in various types of fabrics. For special occasions, the *lungi* is available in the finest cloths and embellished with brocade and embroidery.

Depending on local tradition, *lungis* are tied in various ways. For daily wear, a simple double knot with the ends tucked in at the waist is the most popular, since it is the least likely to slip or come undone. *Lungis* are one of the most practical and comfortable garments, especially for the hot and humid climate of South India.

1-1-2010
1-1-2010
1-1-2010
1-1-2010
O.K.

Far left: *A manager of a tea estate in Munnar wearing colonial British-influenced clothing, khaki bucket shorts, a sleeveless cardigan and a bush hat.*

A selection of lungi-clad men in different regions of South India. Depending on local tradition and the kind of work being done, lungis are tied in different fashions, paired with western-style shirts, or worn with nothing at all.

Left: *Dressed in colour, these tea pickers stand out against Munnar's rolling hills.*

Centre: *A lady bringing her laundry back from the river, making her load look effortless.*

Right: *A lady outside a temple. The sari has certainly been a timeless form of dress. Whether for the young or elderly, for the modern or traditional Indian woman, the sari is the daily attire on all occasions.*

WOMEN

A fascinating aspect of the South India culture is its ancient concept of matriarchal societies. This system was common to many communities in coastal Karnataka and Kerala. A matriarchy is a tradition in which power lies with the eldest mother of a community. True matriarchal societies were and are extremely rare. Wherever human societies have been found, ancient or modern, there has been a marked preference for men to hold the reins of power.

The traditional Nair community in Kerala is matrilinear by system. This meant that the family traced its roots through the women in the family. The children inherited the property of their maternal family. However in today's modern world, this system is rarely practiced.

Besides property and inheritance, matriarchy was also about the celebration of femininity and motherhood. In South Indian literature and philosophy, women are considered to have *shakti*, the power of the feminine. A woman is regarded as auspicious since her shakti protects and empowers her family and community.

The status of women has been subject to many great changes over the past few hundred years. From equal status with men in ancient times, through low points during the medieval period to the promotion of equal rights by many dynamic reformers over the past two hundred years and more, the history of women in India has been eventful.

Far left: *A young lady having her hair combed by her aunt.*

Left: *Even the simplest of cotton saris is a work of art. A lady in Pondicherry.*

T.N.20.Y.3864

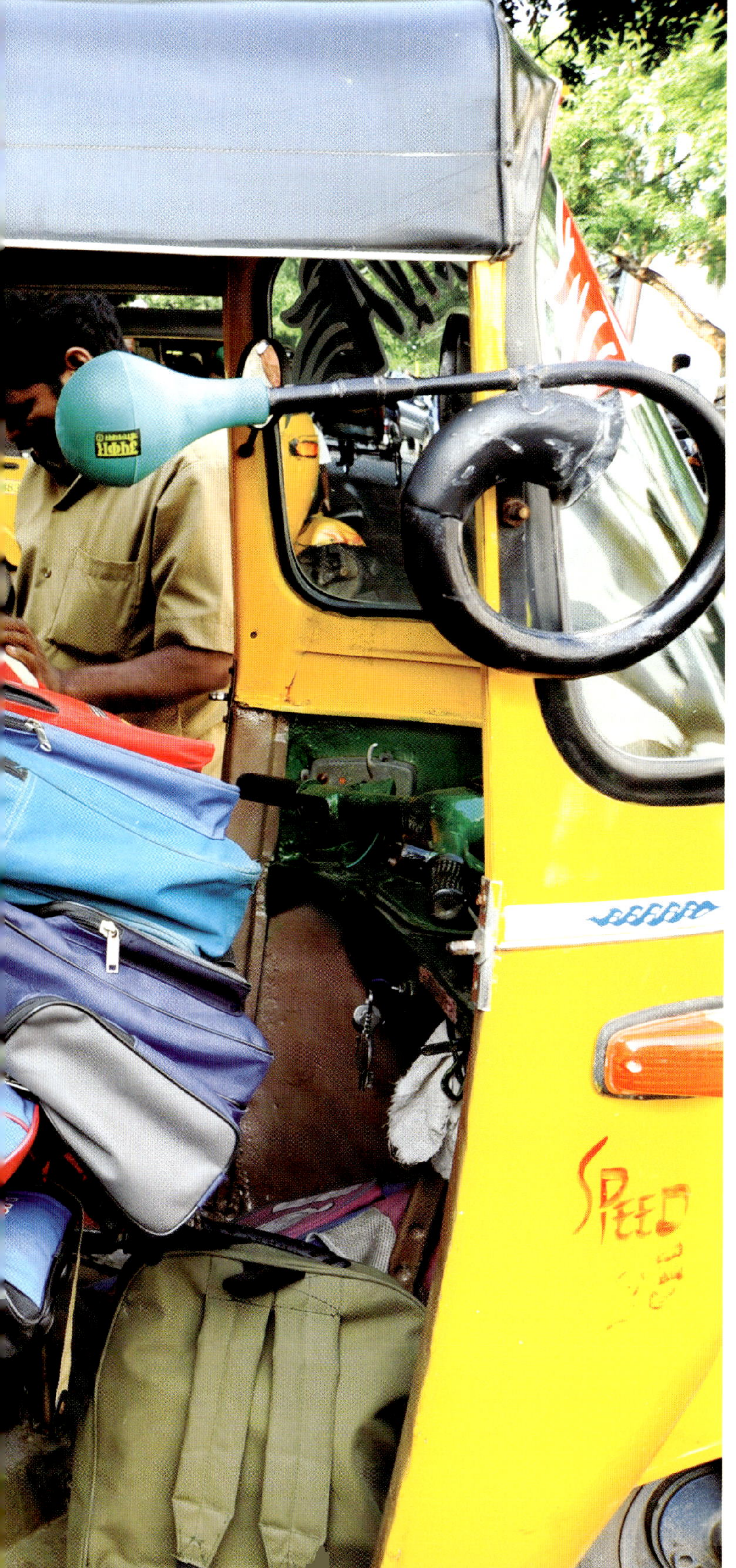

A typical scene in urban Chennai; a three-wheeler piled high with school bags and bursting with excited children returning home from school.

SCHOOL CHILDREN

Children in India get to school on foot, by rickshaw, by bicycle, by bullock-cart, cars or by school bus. They walk across bamboo bridges, navigate noisy city streets teeming with traffic, or trek through forests. The schools they go to are just as varied. School can be a city classroom, a railway platform, or even a walk through nearby hills.

A lot is being done on paper to encourage children from poor rural families to get an education. Free and compulsory education to all children from ages six to fourteen is a constitutional commitment in India. The Parliament of India passed the Right to Education Act (updated in 2009) and became one of a hundred and thirty-five countries to make education a fundamental right of every child. But the basic infrastructure in these small schools is

Children dressed impeccably in their school uniforms lined up to go on a school outing.

more than inadequate. Due to limited resources most schools only have a blackboard in the name of infrastructure.

The Indian government has banned child labour to ensure that children do not enter unsafe working conditions. However, both free education and the ban on child labour are difficult to enforce due to economic disparity and social conditions. Within the Indian states, Kerala has shown the

highest literacy rate at 90 per cent, largely due to its matriarchal pattern of society, and the value it places on education. Every person above the age of seven who can read and write in any language is said to be literate. Here local government leaders have acknowledged that an infant's health depends on the care taken by a mother during pregnancy which in turn depends on her education and on the health and education of her community.

Many young girls and students in South India wear a half-sari as their school uniform; a long skirt, blouse and a dupatta *tied around the waist and draped across the left shoulder like a sari* pallu. *This is a comfortable and suitable style of dressing, especially for the hot climate in the south.*

A group of students have found a quiet spot to study in the eighth-century Kailasnatha temple as Nandi, Shiva's bull and temple guardian, looks on at Kanchipuram, Tamil Nadu.

Facing page (left): *Young boy scouts on their way home.*

Facing page (right): *Schoolgirls wait for their ride to school.*

A group of school children packed into a three-wheeler.

Young girls in the countryside on their way to school.

Cardboard cut-outs of screen celebrities line Marina Beach in Chennai , waiting to be photographed with their fans.

SUNDAY AT THE BEACH

Top: *Mother and daughter enjoying the sea .*

Bottom: *Two young policewomen keep watch.*

Facing page (top): *The young and old visit the beach in their Sunday best.*

Facing page (bottom left): *A mobile street food vendor parked on the sand, selling mouth-watering snacks.*

Facing page (bottom right): *Candy-floss sellers roam the beach.*

CHENNAI
PANIPURI SAMOSA SUNDAL

A young acrobat performing mind-boggling feats on a tightrope.

HOTEL RESOURCE GUIDE

TAJ CONNEMARA
Binney Road
Chennai 600 002, India
Tel: +91 44 6600 0000
www.tajhotels.com

GRT TEMPLE BAY BEACH RESORT
Mamallapuram 603 104, India
Tel: + 91 44 2744 3636
www.grttemplebay.com

HOTEL DE L'ORIENT
17, Rue Romain
Pondicherry 605 001, India
Tel: +91 413 234 3067
www.neemranahotels.com

KAILASH BEACH RESORT
Poornankuppam Village
Ariankuppam Commune
Pondicherry 605 007, India
Tel: +91 413 261 97 00 03
www.kailashbeachhotel.in

THE BANGALA
Devakottai Road, Senjai
Karaikudi 630 001, India
Tel: +91 4565 220 221
www.thebangala.com

THE GATEWAY HOTEL
Pasumalai, Madurai 625 004, India
Tel: +91 452 2371 601
www.tajhotels.com/gateway

AMBADY ESTATE
3rd Mile
Pallivasal P.O.
Munnar, Kerala, India
Tel: +91 4864 0 278361
www.ambadyestate.com

COCONUT LAGOON
Kumarakom Kottayam 686 563
Kerala, India
Tel: +91 481 252 4491
www.cghealth.com

KUMARAKOM LAKE RESORT
Kumarakom North
Kottayam 686 566
Kerala, India
www.thepaul.in

BRUNTON BOATYARD
Fort Cochin 682 001
Kerala, India
Tel: +91 484 221 5461
www.cghearth.com

MALABAR HOUSE
1/269 PARADE ROAD
FORT COCHIN 682 001
Kerala, India
www.malabarhouse.com

ISLA 'LOULOU' VAN DAMME
PANCHAVATTI
Corjuem Island
Aldona, Bardez
Goa 403508, India
www.islaingoa.com

TAJ HOLIDAY VILLAGE
Sinquerim, Bardez
Goa 403 519, India
Tel: +91 832 664 5858
www.tajhotels.com

TAJ MAHAL PALACE TOWER
Apollo Bunder
Mumbai 400 001, India
Tel: +91 22 6665 3366
www.tajhotels.com

About the book

Between the Malabar and Coromandel Coast lie the Southern states of India, once collectively known as Dravida, derived from the Sanskrit word 'drava' (sea). Journey through swaying palm trees and lush waterways, snake shrines and tea plantations shrouded in mist – these visual treats are just a few examples of what South India has to offer. Explore an enchanted mosaic of shore temples, spice markets, painted dancers and Kalari martial artists.

South India, A Mosaic, will evoke powerful sensations of a distinctly magical land, steeped in a wealth of traditions and a dynamic history; an inspiration for people across the world.

About the authors

Melba Levick has done over 50 photography books on travel, design, architecture and gardens in Europe, the Americas and India. Her work has been exhibited and appears frequently in magazines worldwide. Her two most recent books on India are *India Sublime, Princely Palaces of Rajasthan,* and *India Colour*. As a result of these works, she was awarded best photographer on India-Worldwide for 2009 by the Indian Ministry of Tourism. www.melbalevickphotos.com

Ameeta Nanji is an author, artist, and yoga teacher. Educated in Kenya and then in London at the Chelsea School of Art, Ameeta has travelled extensively throughout India, her country of origin. In collaboration with award-winning photographer Melba Levick and art historian Mitchell Crites, she has co-authored two books, *India Sublime* (2007) and *India Colour* (2008). Ameeta currently lives and works in Venice, California. www.ameetananji.com

Ameeta and Melba in Munnar